Copyright © 2017 by Adam Siwiec

All rights reserved

Printed in the United States of America

When The Lights Go Out

The Stories of Another Man

By Adam Siwiec

To the ones that hurt.
To the ones that can't sleep at night because they know that something is wrong with the world.
To the ones that realize perfection is impossible.
To the ones that embrace all perspectives.
To the ones that sacrifice to love.
To the ones that cry.
To the ones that laugh.
To the ones that smile.
To all the fireworks that nobody cares to watch.

Special thanks to God above all else.

Thanks to everyone that helped me write this book.
You know who you are.

Fireworks in the Night Sky 5

She Left Nothing 111

Domestic Gold 166

Fireworks in the Night Sky

You promised to take me to the Stars
The Moon
The Suns

but we've already gone farther

The flames lick the edge of my heart
Oh the afterburn is going to hit me hard
Bring the temperature down
Put you on the Backburner

Backburner

Why can't we just be organic
Who says we have to be like this
Have to do that
Who says we have to prove to each other
Proof is for The Scientist
Not for the lovers

The Scientist

You brought out the best in him
You were the light
That buzzed all around him
Hoping that he would absorb your wild

Neon Halo

For the first time ever
I let the fire in my heart out
And I scorched the world

You ran across the world
As if there was a fire in your step
Or was it your soul?

Orchestra of Flames

Who needs time machines
When you have memories

Time Travelers

The most underrated poems

Lyrics

I flip through dictionaries
Looking for words that describe you
I hesitate in the B's G's and the W's
But I still can't find a fitting word

Let's make our own language

You keep me fresh
I heave a sigh of relief
Whenever I see you
Because I know that
There is always a
New adventure
About to begin

Pine Needles

Mahogany timber splintered through my bones
The chestnut wood cracked on the open fire
The ebony coffee kept your Brown Eyes open
Milk chocolate melted in my pocket
Those caramel almonds crunch in your beautiful ivories
My hazel eyes can do nothing but stare

Brown Eyes

When the Sun
Rises in the West
Sets in the East
You know your world has been turned upside down

Sunshine

I call you at 12:39 am
I come pick you up in my truck
We drive and drive
We park the car at the edge of the trees
I take your hand and guide you to the barbed wire
We jump over
You raise a finger to your lips
And say *hush darling*

The Watchman lies asleep under his light post
We sneak under his nose
And climb to the top of the tower
We watch the full moon
Until the moon says its crowning goodnight

The Watchman

No one is down to earth
When you are down on earth

Falling Star

Remember that time when we got those wintergreen mints
And traveled out to the dark Ozark mountains
We put them between our pearly whites
Then chomped down
We watched as the green lights sparked from our teeth

Remember that time when our hearts Glowed In The Dark?

Glow In The Dark

I want to pick you up
Carry you In My Arms
Then place you on my shoulders
I want to open your eyes
Then point to the mountains, oceans, and castles all around us
And say
"Look. There is a bigger world waiting for us out there"

In My Arms

She could take away your breath
Faster than the wind could take away your warmth

Blizzard

The dirt crunched beneath the tread of my boots
The saloon was abandoned
But the piano still played the same tune with invisible fingers
A Lone Ranger stood in front of the prison
His spurs and revolver glinted in the bloody sun's light
"So you're the new sheriff in town?" He chuckled
"I guess so," I replied

At the end of the road she stood there
She wore a dress that reminded me of a mountain of spiraling clouds
What drew me into this Ghost Town?

Ghost Town

I would get that tingle in my skin
Whenever she gave me that look
I guess I gave her that look back too
Because electricity only runs when two ends meet

High Voltage

She spoke like she was mad
A blast of a revolver
And 6 crystal bullets flew at me
Her Language is crazy
Maybe someday I can speak her tongue
Maybe someday I will understand

But that day is in a galaxy far far away

Her Language

He wasn't looking for love
He was looking for blood

Target

He brought a knife to a gunfight
She brought a pen to a dogfight
Underwhelmed, but capable

Warfare

Laugh like nobody's listening
Smile like nobody's smiling
Radiate like nobody's business
Love him like nobody's watching

It's only you and him

It's as if the world couldn't tell us apart
Our light and shadow combined
And all they saw was a milky moon
As we danced the night away

Dance on the Moon

I looked in your eyes
I saw a never ending reflection of heartbreak and love

Perpetual Waltz

I took you to my favorite place
All I brought with me was a dictionary
We challenged ourselves to define every word in the
English language

Apple
Balcony
Carnivore
Devious
Electorate
Flagella
Gumball
Havoc
Icicle
Jester
Kitten

Then we reached love
We choked and became speechless

Words of Life

I wasn't alive until I met you
I was a corpse looking for a reason
A lost sailboat washed ashore
Waiting for someone to lift his sails
And fly through the hovering door
I thought I had mastered the world
But then I realized
I could never master you
I shivered in the scarlet moonlight
Hoping that someone would be beside me to keep me warm
It's easy to warm your hands
When you live inside someone's heart

Élan Vital

My hands quiver inside of my pockets
My eyes flicker like a wolf in pursuit
My feet freeze beneath a melted soul
The lion thunders and challenges me under the moon's eye
But my mouth can't spill the words you deserve

Paranoid

She slept by me all night
Her arms wrapped around my waist
She could feel my heart race as I progressed through my dreams
And in the morning
She kissed me on my forehead
As if to say:
I had seen everything
And I am there for you

I want to show you my favorite spots
The secret places that only live in my eyes and your dreams
I want you to shimmer underneath the oak trees
I want to take your breath away
Then breath into your heart
Take away all the pain
Turn it into a memory
Wipe away all the tears
Turn it into a jewel that makes you happy until the day you die

Footprints in the Breeze

Whenever I felt down
You would hug me
It felt like the whole world was wrapping her arms around this tiny boy
But the whole world doesn't care who I am

Only You Do

We are both building a tower of hands
We are using our hands to try to disarm each other
We keep trying to outplay each other
We are beating around the bush
One day that tower is going to come crumbling down
We are going to cry so hard

But we still have a chance to stop this

Today
Let's dismantle this tower built out of us
Let's remove our hands
Instead, let's use them to brush away the hair blocking the other's eyes

Tonight
Let's use our hands to wipe away the tears from each other's eyes

This way neither of us will lose this game called life

Jenga

Love is not what you want out of someone
Love is not comprised out of lust, greed, or an urge to be something special
Love does not cause stress, anxiety, or intimidation
Love doesn't break your heart
Love doesn't destroy, separate, or polarize
You can't want love
You can't manufacture love

Love is made out of an acceptance of who someone is
Love realizes that things get tough
But love always has your back
Love is crafted through the memories you create with another person
Love is the bond that rejuvenates souls and calms hurricanes
Love is the indisputable equalizer of the world
Love urges people to laugh and to live and to dream
Love is natural
It's organic
You can't just create love
You nurture it
You grow it
You care for someone
They care for you
You share your life
And you receive a life in return

Two people don't realize how much they are in love with each other, until together they shine bright enough to light up the whole world

That's what love is

You took me back to square one
Made me zoom out
And realize how dull and lifeless the world would be
without you

Colors

The only time I cry
Is when the lights go out
And your head is still pressed against me

Together

Try staring a Magician in the eye
They become agitated and volatile
They know their castles are crumbling into lies

Magician

If you ever want to go dancing in the rain, call me
 Thunder and Lightning
We can glide hand-in-hand
The sideways rain wafts between our feet
We flash across the sky
Carving our own paths
We strike the ground with our alabaster spears
Create a forest fire in the desert of green
We spew our endless tears
Comforted by the cacophony of a resounding symphony

When we are a Thunderstorm, people notice

Thunderstorm

He had only ever wanted to love
She had only ever wanted to fly

Tangled in the Sky

What's the probability of me finding you?
One in seven billion

chi squared

Give me your canyons
And I can make a mountain
Give me your rivers
And I can make a city

Real Life

She didn't let the monsters kill her
But she still remembers them
She showed me her Jungle Book

Jungle Book

If I could freeze you right now
The world would see a comet shoot across the sky

Frozen Star

Everyday, I see something new in your eyes
And it's not the part of you that I hadn't known about

It's the part of you that neither of us have discovered before

Part of You

Look up, you can see the dazzling turquoise sky

Look up, you can't walk straight by looking at your feet

Look up, there is a place you are supposed to be

Look up, you are on Angel's Roof

Angel's Roof

He lost his sight
On the sunniest day

Sunshine Thief

You asked me why I stay up late

Up On Magic

I picked up that old sepia picture of us
You captioned it "2 scoops of infinity"

Memories

We dipped our fingers in the sand
Twirled them until they couldn't breath
We slept in that sand
Drunk on each other eyes

We never went home that day

Somedays I'm just madly in love with you
On the other days
I'm still madly in love you

Perpetual

If I found you in this small Town
~~Imagine what I could find in the city~~
Nothing could ever compare with you

Town

I am a free man
Enslaved by my dreams

I am a prisoner of war
Liberated only by her

Sugar Skull

Even when the sun is covered
His rays still seem to bend
To get to her heart

Solar Eclipse

They covered my words
When your eyes needed them the most

Smother

Jump out of an airplane

Pop

Sleep on Machu Picchu's grass

Pop

Hammock in Stonehenge

Pop

We have a lot more to go

Crystalline Bubbles

Whenever I try to stop thinking about you
My mind always wanders back
It's like you're magnetic

Cobalt

The doctor looks in your ear
"Stick out your tongue"
"Ahhhhhh"
"There is nothing wrong with you"

But I know what's wrong
Take some of my Typewriter Serum

Typewriter Serum

I dropped my Nutella sandwich in the Tennessee Snow
Ma! You might want to see this!
I screamed and ran back inside
Ma got up and looked out the window

A ring of maroon ash circled the backyard
A red tinge plastered the fence and surrounding obstacles
Streaks of bronze dispersed from the center of the collision

I brought up my courage to creep into the unnatural circle
I reached the middle and saw a baroque object
A brilliant opal ring

I picked it up cautiously

What is it? Ma asked, unable to see clearly
Uhhhhhh, just a piece of rubble, I responded
I stealthily slipped the ring into my pocket, not wanting to draw attention

Tennessee Snow

Rolling clouds grasp the victim by the ear
Cacophony of silence
The diligent earth bows to its elevated king
The zephyr's grip strength wavers

Chasing the Wilted Fog

The trampled ghosts sit beside me
They whisper these crazy thoughts in my ears
I sip a small latte
Inside of my cocoon
But the ghosts of dawn won't leave me alone

Empty Coffee House

Remember that time I laughed?
Neither do I
The merchandise of my youth
The organic, thriving laughter
Buried in this earth
Enveloped by the sands of time
Decayed into this untapped gasoline

But you
You perforated those years
And sparked all that I had left so long ago

Untamed Obsidian

Time doesn't tick
It slurs

Where Palms Blink

He tries to divert your beat
He tries to pick you up and drop you in a place that you do not belong
He tries to open you up and mess with the gears inside of you
"I'm trying to fix a broken clock," he says

But please
Never become one of his Copycat Metronomes

Copycat Metronome

I can fall asleep every night
Knowing that your words will still be cradling my head at daybreak

Goodnight

How do you stop a torrent of rain?
You don't
Just make sure that nobody drowns in the aftermath

Deluge

If Nikes could talk
They would tell me of the time you tried to run away from home

If Nikes could talk
They would tell me about how much weight you have lost

If Nikes could talk
They would tell me your ticklish spots

If Nikes could talk
They would repeat the insane slurs yelled at you

If Nikes could talk
They would replay your highest jump

If Nikes could talk...

Take my last breath
Turn it into a million words

Fantasize

It was the first time you had flown on an airplane
You repeatedly chanted under your breath "Don't let me die... Don't let me die..."
Your hand was gripping mine with the strength of 10 rhinoceroses

We landed and exited the plane
You didn't sleep at all on the 12 hour flight
I remember your sweaty palms had gripped mine the whole trip
And I never let go

The Doves of Oslo

Drown out the waves
Listen to my symphony of silence

Focus

When you look me in the eye
You look into the gentle eye of a hurricane

Hurricane Blink

You asked me if I care about you

I keep you in my prayers at night
Oh I care
I care a lot

Hardship

She was the shade of magic
That only I could paint

Paint

She asked me so many questions
I gave her all the wrong answers

Q and A

Looking up at the stars
I had a massive realization
That I am just an Adam in the Universe

The Atom

My secret is now our secret
Or is it just our story?

Enigma

If I could show the world your words laid down for me
Like little puzzle pieces
What would you want them to see?

Mosaic

A beautiful person is one who rises proudly with all the bloody scars

Not an unblemished person who has never fallen in the face of pain

Beauty

You asked me, which poems are the best
I answered, the ones that write themselves

Elves in the Night

Dear Dinosaurs,

How could the whole universe
Be meant for me

Sincerely,
A (Bewildered) Atom

Seconds don't last forever
Words last millennia
Don't let the words bleach away your charismatic shine
You have a long life ahead of you my beautiful Nova

Corrupt Nova

If words can change a life
And books can change the world
What could change the universe?

He clambered down from the stars above
He came to rescue you
To run away with you
And take you to a new home

The Castaway from Ursa Major

Graffiti infects her tendons
The exhaust of her breath ripples in the clouded air
Each compartment tells of her story
The rails keep her steadfast in pursuit of the destination

The Iron Horse

Manifest a bond that can never be broken
Use the hammer in your hand to build crimson galaxies
So that whenever I look up at the night sky
I can never forget you

Hammer

Let's study the world together
Maybe we will realize
We can change the world
Hand-in-hand
With our endless hearts

Limitless

The reason I saved you was because
I knew I couldn't save myself

It was too late
To cover my own mistakes

But you had a second chance
And that second chance
 It was me

Painting White Walls With White Paint

"Wake up! It's time to explore"
You shook awake my dreams from hibernation
And took them by the hand

You showed them the caverns, the mountains, the lay of the land
The calico apricot trees and the cobblestone streets
They got a taste of Adventure
A taste of exploration

Now we must feed them some real life memories

Real Life Adventures

I am standing in a quicksand desert
Shifting waves of desperation flutter on the horizon
This is my last shot to show you truth
~~However, if I fail~~

What if I told you that I have been telling the truth my whole life?

Someday You Will Remember My Quicksand Reminders

Lies are boring
If you want adventure, take a dose of truth

Genuine Deception

Whenever I got stuck
You got stuck with me, so that I wouldn't be lonely

The Principles of Friendship

She had just enough spark
To ignite a blaze

Call 911

My grandfather always told me
Anticipate, anticipate, anticipate

But you hit me like a meteor

Anticipating Infinity

When the world is moving at the speed of light
I can still see your smile
Frozen by happiness

The Speed of Light

He seemed like a nice guy
Until you realized
He would sink you
If he didn't get what he wanted

Sailor By Day, Pirate By Night

You took me to the ocean side
"Look. You can see the fish swimming"

But all I saw was the reflection of two crazy wild dreamers

The Sailboats of Marseille

The river of tears in my eyes
They nourish a plant that does not accept donations

Crying to Dead Roses

You asked me:
If you had one wish, what would it be?
I responded:
I wish I could fly

But deep in my head, I wished to run away with you

Two Fireworks in the Night

You harmoniously resonate with the whole world
Yet you are still a perfect pitch

Lullabyes

Put simply:
It wasn't that she couldn't handle the world
The world just couldn't handle her

I want to tell you everything
But if I did
I would suffocate you with words

There Is No Gold At The End Of The Rainbow

She was a piece of dark chocolate
In a world so artificially sweet
She was genuine nectar
In a world that sipped blood for celebration

Candy Girl

How about all those times when you thought your problems were solved?
Did you not feel free in those moments?
You told me that you could fly on angel's wings
But why not use your own?

I grew up in this place called the Land of the Lost
I shook the same hands, walked the same dirt

But then she wandered into this lonely town
And in her back pocket
She had a map
A map to myself

Land of the Lost

I hope that in your darkest times
In your ravenous pain
In your indescribable suffering

You will reach in your pocket and hold that brilliant opal ring
And know that I am always here for you

When the creases in our hands multiply
And the canyons in our skin erode
And we can't even speak the words "I love you"
I know our hearts will still pump the same ferocious blood
of our youth

The color of your heart is
one million rainbows
blended inside
Those 4 pulsating chambers

Some Emotions Are Too Great to be Shared

She was not the woman that would leave you stranded alone
Whenever a tsunami started to rise from the depths of a dying ocean

The finest memories are the ones that are only shared between two people

Good Memories Are Just Happy Secrets

She Left Nothing

She could creep up on you like a vine
Slowly wrapping her ever lengthening arms around your legs
Then your spine
Then your heart

She could choke you
But it was that slow gentle choke
The kind of choke that you could enjoy
The kind that leaves you smiling in your grave

She could poison you
She was a snake
Constricting and rooting you in her grip
Circling up your torso
Then staring you in the eyes
She would probe your nose with her triangular tongue
Then kiss your lips
As she slowly whispered
"Please, I can't be your last wish"

Fire Phlox

You don't realize you will miss her
Until she is already gone

61 Petals

The sharpest knives are
The ones that
Don't hurt

Paroxysm

Ravishing my veins
Throbbing arteries
My handwriting dilates
As I try to write down my feelings
The feelings of a broken heart
A broken heart that no Chemicals can rectify

Chemicals

A puff of smoke in the air
It drifts into all our noses
Let's dilute this pain together

Secondhand Sadness

How can I tell the difference between your lies and truths?
All your words are illusions

Hallucinations

He packed his suitcase and left
I still remember looking out at him
As he drove away through the fields of gold
He was wearing his fedora and suit
His last words were:

It's hard to forget
The words that she promised me

I remember the day when she came
She glided on a flat boat constructed of soothing words, a gentle smile, and promises of how she would never lie
She came infected under the radar
She brought a fiery storm of arrows into the civilians living in my heart
She Pillaged me of everything
She destroyed the carefully constructed barriers that I had made to bar myself from the world
She took my body
She took my woes
I didn't want her to cause anymore damage
So I left all my gold on the shore

If he leaves and doesn't look back
He never loved you

If he leaves and says goodbye
And calls you every day
And sends you postcards
And says goodnight
And wants to visit you
He loved you since the day you met

When Eyes Meet

Was I just too much for you?
Did I not fit in the small jar labeled
Bug That Will Die Soon

Lightning in a Jar

Who do you think I am?
A puppet?
Do you think I'm willing to be twisted into submission by you?

Do you think I am as loose as a handful of sand?
Willing to have my values molded by your etched hands

Do you think my age reflects a life of ignorance?
Who do you think I am?
Your Apprentice?

Apprentice

I remember the Real You
That Real smile
Those Real eyes
Those Real laughs

Where'd they go?

The Real You

Those Redwood Trees leave me keeling
Those thin rings reflect the saddest years
But the Tree keeps growing
Nourished by those dry tears

Redwood Tree

The product of cloud
Beats a steady rhythm on the ground
A soft reminder of what is to come
The Prelude of a tornado

Prelude

Why does your face frown
Whenever my face smiles?

Reciprocal

Tsunami of tears stratify my face
You are going to the beaches to resolve a problem you did not deserve
Oceans at Large in our bloody soil
There is no 2nd place when it comes to war

Oceans at Large

I fell for you way too fast
Way too hard

You're going to break my heart someday
And I'm going to break yours too

If we really loved each other
Then we can always tune our broken song

Fallen

It will never become my decision to make a decision to decide what decision you should make in this journey called life
Who are we to make decisions anyway?

I came upon a pool of crystal clear water
I bent over to take a drink
And saw a girl with long hair staring back at me
I reached up and touched my hair
It was still short
She was a Reflection of my dreams
The girl reached up and touched her hair too
I waved at her and she waved back
I smiled and she beamed
We made a silly face
Then giggled
I reached closer to the water and tried to feel her
She reached closer as well
My fingers brushed the top of the water and I never saw her again

Reflection

It was after all my walls had been torn down
That you saw inside of me
And realized: I care

Don't hold anything back dear
Everyone moment of spilled sunshine
Leaves scars etched into my heart

All Your Light Can Save Me

You made the whole world spin faster
Or maybe it's just because I'm falling
Falling with a tear in my heart

Give Me Your Parachute

There was no love
To tie down
Your paper-weight words
To my heart

There was no love
To pull me up
Out of the waters
To dry my tears

There was no love
To hold my hand
To tell me that everything was alright
To tell me that everything would be ok

There was no love

Learn to heal when you sense the rain
Learn to feel when you hear the pain

Cloudy Heart

I feel drowned
When you drench me with nothing

Empty Rain

Let's both pretend like we are confused
So that we don't have to admit that emotion
What's it called?
It falls somewhere between love and enthused

Guilt, That's It

I'm always afraid that whenever I see your eyes
It will be the last time
I'm scared that I will forget to say goodbye

I hope that whenever you look in my eyes
You don't see the eyes
Of the ghosts
Of your
Past

Because I Might Just Close Them

Don't fall in love with someone you potentially could love

Because no one ever lives up to their potential

Keep an eye on someone that could potentially make you a better person
That could potentially push you toward your dreams
That could potentially uphold your standards
That could potentially make you laugh
That could potentially make you cry
That could potentially hold your hand

And once they have done all those things
They are not potential anymore
They are reality

And that's the moment when you can let everything go
And love them with your whole, unpending heart

She was the one who hurt me the most
I put so much care into her
That she got scared and ran away
She took a piece of me
And never gave it back

I don't know why she got scared
She ran away

He would interrupt you
Cut through your words
Until he left you with nothing
Except for the shredded alphabet

Knives Only Divide

You are like a stoplight
You always remind me when to go

I came to fix all your problems
But when I left
I had fixed all my own

Did I fix yours?

You are the gas I breathe everyday

You are the poison I sip every night

You are the venom that courses through my veins

But I still feel alive

Zyklon B

It's after the war has been lost
That you will realize the torture in my side
Yet I still dream of ways to understand your pain
I will wait while the blood dries
Because all we ever do is say goodbye

Heartbreak Warfare

You became the dumping ground
For the selfish slander of a disillusioned dynasty

You became the dumping ground
For the words that nobody claimed to own

You became the dumping ground
For the weight of the world

You became the dumping ground
That bristled with energy
Waiting to implode

You became the dumping ground

The chime dinged as I walked into the shop
I sat down to grab a cup of coffee
I had never liked coffee when I was young
But it was an acquired taste like they say

Then this lady sat down next to me and we just started talking
I felt like I could tell her anything, everything
I started talking about this girl I knew when I was young
About how strong and independent she was
And how she had her own plans
Then the lady whispered,
"And tell me how they used to be. Those things that were you and me"

I looked in her eyes
Then I knew it was her
She was still that evergreen girl
The one that could never grow old

If you just keep moving
Nobody will notice you falter

Darling, just fall as hard as you can
Because my arms will always be there to catch you

Skydive

I'm too scared
To put it all on the line
Hands tied behind my back
Eyes closed
And let you feel my heart

Afraid

I cry your tears
Because no amount of liquid
Can ever fill the emptiness I feel inside my heart

The tears rolled from her eyes
Committing treason on her soft skin
She cried for no reason in general
Only because she felt the weight of the world
In her heart, in her hands, on her back
Rooting her to the ground
Laying her dreams to rest
In a shallow grave

Heavyweight Champ

The tundra of frigid soil lay before him
He came prepared with only whiskey, words, and a shovel
To unearth her frozen body
To steal her buried gems
So he could marvel at
How beautiful her dreams were

The Gravedigger's Handbook

For the moment the air stood still
And started breathing in

Then it opened its eyes
And saw the world as a human being

I swirled the remaining scotch in my glass
And thought of how much it reminded me of you:

Fiery
Bold
And always left me wanting more

Alcoholic

She laid her empty words on the table before her

Lie, 3 points
Pretend, 10 points
Confuse, 12 points
Bluff, 13 points

She made a new highscore

Scrabble

Did anyone ever realize
That the stars look down upon us
And wonder how we got so far away?

I know that it can be hard to put on a smile some days
But just remember
A smile is the only piece of clothing that is free

Yet also priceless

Don't give up on the person that gives everything

The Giving Tree

God places us with the people that will challenge us
That will break us
That will build us

He knows what's best for us and what we need
We should never doubt that

One day we will both look back
And realize all the mistakes we made
And realize what we should've done
But we are living in the present
And the present is always trying to fix the past
Even though it can't
It can change the path
But never erase what happened

Remember in grade school
When you would arrive on the first day of school with a fresh pack of pencils
You would go through 10 in a week but you wouldn't worry because you knew you had more

But when you ran down to that last pencil, you made it last for months

The same applies for love:

Whenever you receive lots of love, you take it for granted because you always expect it to be there.

But once it's all gone, you wish you had been more careful
And maybe appreciated and kept the love you received earlier on

Pencil Love

I gave you 100% of my heart
That was the only thing I had left
But it wasn't enough

I guess hearts have different values

She didn't need Redbull
Or Monster
Or coffee
To keep her awake at night
Her worries were enough

Caffeine

Domestic Gold

Fire dwells within the cave
Flames conquer those who brave
Anger puts kindness in a headlock
Anger holds humanity at bay
But just watch love come creeping in

Anger

Bloody hand dipped in purple paint
Reaches up and shades the foggy window
It spells
Bad things in here
Don't come in

817

I wake up sweating at midnight
The Cold Chills prickle my spine
They crawl like a tarantula into my brain
Those dreadful memories
They still haunt me to this day

Cold Chills

You turned me into a Loose Cannon
I can't help but explode
Take my dust
Turn me into a Phoenix

Loose Cannon

The gifts of generations past
Strewn on the door
The invisible blood
Smeared on my walls
The gashes on the floor
Scratched by a lost soul
My dreams
Lie dusty and folded in the corner
What's under my bed
Is something I dread

My Room is a Mess

Why are we forced to be like things we are not?
Because like diamonds we shine our truth through
Pressure

Pressure

How can you save a man
That has been shot with a barrage of words
Right through the gut?

High Caliber

Years ago
I forgot to hit the brakes
I hit the guy in front of me
Flew off my high horse
It's funny
No one takes the time to smell the asphalt
Until you hate it so badly

The blood, the scars

I wrapped myself in Duct Tape
Head to toe
I vowed to myself
Never let anything in
Never let anything out

Now, not even Duct Tape can hold in the molten lava
Someone needs to catch me in a bucket
Before I melt all over the floor

Duct Tape

The black crow swiveled in his nest
He beat his shriveled wings and ascended into the cloudless air
He was guided only by a moonlit stare

The sun rose the next day
The fox waved its apricot coat in the morning dew
The cricket released a charming new tune

The sun set
The crow descended into a red oak tree
He danced from branch to branch in excitement
He watched as the tree swayed under his weight

This is the time he releases his poison
This is the time that Everything Changes

Everything Changes

The therapist asked
What is your biggest strength?
I pointed to My Ears
What is your biggest weakness?
I pointed to My Ears

My Ears

The pack of wolves surround the lonely elk
A cub watches his fathers from the top of a distant hill
He watches as they grab the elk by the legs
He watches as they jump on the innocent beast
They sink their fangs into its hide
They tear apart pieces of the victim that were never meant to be exposed
They rip and shred and pull and tug
They are hungry monsters fueled by their own desire of hatred, lust, and superiority

The cub wants to be better than them
He wants to show that he is different
That he loves and cares
But he is their son

Torn to Pieces

Someday's I feel like just another statistic
Just another dot on a graph

But how can you cage an endless number?

Pi

I've only heard them twice

I remember the first time...
I was in the attic
I remember there was an unexpected knock at the door
I put my blue dog in the maroon cupboard
And hid under the stairwell
It was dark and cramped
They still found me

The second...
I was working in the factory
The smell of flesh and poison choked all life
The guards started shouting
There was no food that day
Then they came
The saving stars

Guns of August

Think of writing as a weapon:

The words are the bullets
The author is the gun
When decoupled, everybody is safe
But when connections are made
There will be blood and tears

Anonymous Literature

Breath In
Breath Out

You just inhaled the air that all of our ancestors have inhaled
If we all breath in the same air then why are we so different?
The output of our bodies:
Hate, Love
Peace, Violence

Is it just the product of the air we breath?

This Air We Breath

The only time my heart feels anything
Is when people pour their hearts into mine
Then they shake it
And stir it
And let it marinate

Do you want a sip?

Martini In My Heart

Give me a piano
6 firecrackers
A few mints
Maybe a can of spray paint
And a canvas

Then I can describe what is happening in my head

And Maybe a Lighter Too

Am I just two authors under one pen?
Or am I one author with two pens
Simultaneously writing the chronicles of love and chaos?

One Mind, One Heart, One Pen

Rip and split
I dried my hands with ripped dreams

Karate Chopping Paper Towels

He told me
You can change the world
With your own two feet
You can fix any heart
With your soothing smile and words

The Man Who Could Fix Anything

I learned how to play in a room by myself
For 8 years
To simulate how it sounded
To be with the others I had hindered to love

John Mayer's Anthem

Touching one heart
Is a million times greater
Than touching a million hands

Impact

I will never realize just how much He laid down for me
Never

Slashes and Thorns

Options

It makes the wisest hesitant

Opinions

It makes the critics roar

Opportunity

It runs in my veins

It's difficult trying to write about things we don't understand
But we do it anyway

Confiscated Emotions

I cried all the right tears for all the wrong reasons

I've had so many stones pulled from under me
That I just keep building others up
Just so that they can't see how far I've fallen

My Foundation is Your Castle

Life is like flying an airplane
Except the airplane
Has no controls
No engine
No propellor
No wings
No body
No seats

We're just free falling, hoping that somebody catches us

I was trying to follow my path in the darkness
I was tripping and stumbling
So I just sat down and thought:

If I just had a light to guide me
A light to show me

But I do
It's just inside of me

My body died
But my words
They kept on writing

Immortal

Standing on the mountain
I looked down
And I saw more sky than you could ever see looking up

How did I get this far?

I'm just the shadow of a bigger man
I'm just a chick with a small wing-span
I tried to be like you and soar
So I jumped

but I forgot I couldn't fly

Sometimes I forget I'm holding my breath
I just need to breathe out
And then let everything in
Then I can sink to the bottom of the ocean
Where all my kin lie

Sunken Jewels

Even diamonds have imperfections
It's just a matter of time
Before they are noticed

Made in United States
Orlando, FL
05 April 2022